The Itchy Sea

MARK WALDRON
was published by S
appears in *Identity*
published by Bloodaxe
with I

Also by Mark Waldron

POETRY
The Brand New Dark (Salt, 2008)

The Itchy Sea

by

MARK WALDRON

SALT
LONDON

PUBLISHED BY SALT PUBLISHING
12 Norwich Road, Cromer, Norfolk NR27 0AX, United Kingdom

All rights reserved

© Mark Waldron, 2011

The right of Mark Waldron to be identified as the
author of this work has been asserted by him in accordance
with Section 77 of the Copyright, Designs and Patents Act 1988.

This book is in copyright. Subject to statutory exception
and to provisions of relevant collective licensing agreements,
no reproduction of any part may take place without the written
permission of Salt Publishing.

Salt Publishing 2011

Printed and bound in the United Kingdom by Lightning Source UK Ltd

Typeset in Swift 9.5 / 13

*This book is sold subject to the conditions that it shall not,
by way of trade or otherwise, be lent, re-sold, hired out,
or otherwise circulated without the publisher's prior consent
in any form of binding or cover other than that in which
it is published and without a similar condition including this
condition being imposed on the subsequent purchaser.*

ISBN 978 1 84471 827 6 paperback

1 3 5 7 9 8 6 4 2

for Julie

Contents

The Blown	1
The Bead	2
Crocodile	4
Were I to jump	5
The Life Cycle of the Fly	6
One day, many years from now	8
Paris	9
Marcie Outside	10
Marcie in the Dock, Up for Being Juicy	11
WWII Marcie	12
Marcie is Half-Woken	13
The Chocolate Car	14
His Life Lost Him	15
The Arctic Circle is an Ironical Hot-Spot	16
Some Time Afterwards	17
The Limpet	18
A Fire Itself is Quiet	19
Everything	20
Your Hand	21
The Warehouse	22
Take a Gulp of Air	23
I Can Use my Mouth	24
So, I heard and also dreamed	26
Mallards	27
Of Plants	28
To change one dog to one cat	29
And see	30
Iron	33
I stood, preposterous	34
The Moon	35
Dawn	36

Rooms	37
The Attributes of Cutlery	38
I could certainly see you better	39
Of Course, We've All Seen This Kind of Thing Before	41
When You Do This Over and Over	42
Lion	43
Look at the trees which carry on regardless	44
Defenestration	45
Well yes, where we interface	46
The darking sky	47
Skin is the callus	48
If I was	49
Uncertain Voices Roost	50
Inside	51
Observe the likeness of a slab of beef	52
The Sea	53
Beef is Made of Meat and Victory	54
The Petard	55
Make Use of My Poem in Any Way You Like	57
Taste	58
Rude	60
And there he is again	61
Grub	63
Poem for Us	64
In the end	65
The Porcelain Dog	66

Acknowledgements

Some of these poems, or versions of them, have appeared in *Magma*, *Pen Pusher*, *Poetry London*, *Rising*, *The Pocket Spellbook* (Sidekick Books 2010) and the *2010 Shuffle Anthology*.

I'd like to thank John Stammers and Roddy Lumsden for their advice on these poems, as well as my wife, Julie, for her always invaluable opinions.

The Itchy Sea

The Blown

The itchy sea,
being eternally discomfited,
seeks an original arrangement

which might restore its calm,
though with each adjustment
it leaves that resolution further behind.

And the thickish, strewn and ravelled
wind which we imagine blown
is sucked towards the spools on which

it would be kempt and reeled,
as a man is shevelled red and raw
about the brittle sticks of him.

The Bead

It was on a business trip in Hungary
that I happened upon something particular:
the plainest mundanity protruding
from the shell it usually inhabits,
as the fleshy foot of a razor clam
may stick, tongue-like, from it's brittle tube
when it is unafraid, or as rude marrow
might extrude from a blown bone.
(That is always how the everyday
is caught unmasked, not, as one might expect,
teaming rampantly underneath its stone,
or squeaking clean like a shaven bear
stood shivering on the forest's uncertain fringe.)
A few of us were sitting in the hotel bar,
when Ray remarked he'd eaten minestrone
for his supper, and told us he'd discovered,
sitting in the bottom of his bowl,
a blue bead. Caitlin said, in that dry,
ironic tone that comes upon a people
in a time of deathly peace, *Well,
you're definitely the winner of something, Raymond.*
And Ray muttered that he'd pushed it
down the back of the sofa.
Some six months later I resolved
to go back for that bead. For when our work
in Hungary was done, and we'd returned
to our homes and reversed ourselves
back inside our callous lives, I found
I couldn't forget it. I pictured it, as you do now,
at first pale grey to the touch, among

the brittle bits of dirt and dust
in the lightless gutter of its resting place,
and then bright blue as I brought it, gleaming,
to the surface. And the more I pictured it,
the more the fact of its existence became exquisitely
arousing to me. Yes, certainly that busy seed
had stuck its roots down into my mind
until they would have taken
my whole troubled ego with them had I yanked
that gorgeous portion of the plant
that was now quite visible above the surface
of my dreams, and soon some unfamiliar gumption
began to coalesce around the tickling
irritation of those roots, until I found
I'd formed a plan (a plan which I
will never action): to travel back to Hungary,
to the hotel in the small town where,
pretending I've lost a valuable ring
(which I'd describe in some pedantic detail),
I'd ask permission of the inscrutable manager,
before I press my nearly blinded fingers down
the back of the sofa. I'd know for certain then,
what I will never know,
the extent to which I am my own ghost.

Crocodile

It's been observed by small children of a certain lineage
and temperament and style of education,
that a house is comparable to a croc

whose back suggests brick; whose teeth call to mind
the white painted bars on the nursery windows; whose intentions
sway rhythmically as landings vacillate outside rooms,

and whose actions are the contents of the house, so that
a wardrobe is a slow submerging, and small key in a kitchen drawer
is a breath pushed into the tedious river—

an exhalation, the bubbles of which, on reaching air,
will open wide as mouths of tiny hippopotami, to cough
their weedy coughs and let go the ordinary smell of human peace.

Were I to jump

or to fall, or were I pushed to my death
from a high window of an apartment block,

or from the edge of a cliff,
then, at the end of that fall, the ground will act

like a sieve, keeping my flesh and bones to itself,
as well as my clothing and any other belongings

which I may have about me,
such as my keys, coins and wristwatch,

while my soul (which I am riddled with)
will continue its downward journey for a little distance

(perhaps for a metre or so, depending on the height
of the preceding drop).

And then, relieved of its hot nest,
it will wear on its face the most abject expression,

not that of the exposed oyster as it's sucked, sobbing
from its shell, but rather,

that which the fledgling wears underneath its feathers,
when it takes its flapping plunge into maturity.

The Life Cycle of the Fly

The housefly on the ceiling,
his maggot does the thinking.
His maggot is the undried fly,

the dreamy fly that lives inside
the black and brittle crate,
and is its creamy pilot.

He swells himself on levers
to make the wings buzz,
to make the legs go,

to move the rough eyes about,
to send out the long lips,
and make himself seen by that

pappy grub of the other sex,
who's loose inside her derelict,
washed-up box of blackened wood;

though the glint of her, a glimpse
of her white give is given
through the timber's winking split.

Before she was boxed
and grey ribbon-bowed with wings,
the maiden maggot writhed

as though she was in pain
and fit to pop. She seemed to mean
to throw her own self off herself,

or to take issue with her own will,
or to find the air disgusting,
but in fact, she was laughing

and her entire body was her smile,
her smile being all teeth,
the segments each a tooth.

I loved you as that maggot
that you were, and licked,
you shone like one.

You were not yet the fly
you would become,
the mourning-black contraption

which arises on the other side
of the pupa's brown casket
to carry off the cargo

of her doughy soul.
How bleak she looks, the fly,
uncovered as she is by gloss,

ensconcing as she does
all the burnished lacquer
of her worm.

One day, many years from now

A winter or a summer or a spring or autumn day, such as
the day the hordes in pointed helms ran like runny honey
through the broken walls of Suceava as the treacherous

and faux-fainting trees let go their pretty leaves
like flirting ladies dropping handkerchiefs, and the whole
of the ruined sky rolled beneath the table to continue

in succumbing to its precious wounds alone.
One day such as that day when the ground gave up
the ground, the sticks, the tree to the immense

uncomplicated army with its single thought and single heart
and single heat and single dung of many parts
that were left strewn across the overlooking hills

like the bitty, broken dirt of sheep. One day such as that
forgiven day, or such as this, or such as any other, I'm afraid
you might begin to wonder where you were in all of this.

Paris

I keep finding you again, forcing my trodden face into the light
that's like a closed door. Sometimes the city pulls itself down.
Sometimes the city crunches up into day.

Most of the time I'm copying people, but that's my business;
well, apart from the fact that I'm copying you too.
I'm copying you so that later I will be able to predict

where you might go, and then be there when you get there
wearing this told-you-so smile. We used to go to Paris
that rancoured in its glory, its age like pain, its feet on the sky.

We walked in it together, in the stone genitals of a woman.
Light is, as old dark was. And things are, it turns out,
quite what they seem. Truth is, I have never understood;

the whole of this moves away from me when I get close to it;
perhaps there's only people driven seemingly into the ground,
and the self with its soul that looks like the glass in a mirror.

We're all hanging on to the world's uncomfortable surface,
and between us and rock is the thin skin of soil. I shan't talk
about how hot it can be deeper, underneath the rock.

I'll spare you that. Black-hot under Paris. So, this is my self
that hangs about on its own face like a teenager loitering
on a low wall, or like a mood.

Opening my own pod-like eyes, I get inside them and look out.
See: reflected on the curve of them is you in Paris, twice;
and under that, just clear jelly and a lens stiffening with age.

Marcie Outside

She betrays the soft odour
of something beautifully wrapped and then unwrapped

and smelt and then wrapped up again,
and then unwrapped again and smelt again and so on;

I say she has the atmosphere of a small hole stuck in paper
with a pin,

a hole that's been made and then made and then made etc.,
as though the maker had been

each time thrilled to pieces with his work;
she displays the flossed, pre-sweetened *déjà vu* of the alive.

Marcie in the Dock, Up for Being Juicy

Marcie's curly wig,
which irritates rather than tickles the judge,

is made of the hair of a dead 'un.
All Rise.

I'd like to refer you, m'lud, to this what follows:
First off, Marcie's essential goodies:

a smile in its birthday suit, creeping backwards
out of her unencountered mouth;

her tasty, reversible shout; her actual smell
(which had once slid off my purchaseless love

and fallen about her and now hangs off the end
of her exact and squeaky shooting match)

and second: all the undescribed glory
of which the well-tooled day itself is made.

WWII Marcie

It's May 1942. Marcie is standing on the roof with her brother.
She's watching the bombers droning over. There is, as there was,
a certain shifting softness about the whole tableau.

Historical Marcie is twenty, and the vision is absolutely running off her,
pouring off her so you'd need a chain of men, working hard,
working fast with buckets, to catch it, to collect it as it cascades

down towards the ground. Serious, helmeted men they are,
and they're working for me. And the portion that escapes,
which they can't catch with their clumsy metal pails

(whose convex rims they hold respectfully against
the convex shapes of her body), *that* part gets over their gloves
and their heavy boots and their pants and the surface of the flat roof,

so that one man slips in it and falls, and then they all turn and look
at me, the men, and laugh, and now even Marcie is laughing,
and her brother, and then I turn and laugh at me too and I sit down

on purpose in the slightly viscous wet, before the bombers, having done
their job, their loads now lightened, turn and disappear eastwards,
gaining altitude in the hot air that rises from the raging city.

Marcie is Half-Woken

The rippled sheets bring her to her limbs
and then her hands.
She is tugged up part way to wakefulness,

just half-topped with charm and light,
as committed to preparedness as a semi-on,
she owns that same chill torridity that pops

bang off the middle, just as one far off day
the clunking Earth will cup in its core
a fading hub of warmth smaller than an egg.

The Chocolate Car

The little chocolate car has bodywork like a sweet wrapper
and no wheels or windows. Everything inside the car's bodywork

is made of chocolate. The engine, the battery, the cables and pipes,
the fuel, the oil, the water, the break fluid, the steering wheel,

the gear stick, the handbrake, the foot controls, the rear-view mirror,
the seats and seat belts, the sweet wrappers in the door compartments,

the door compartments, the driver, the passengers, their innards,
their flesh and their blood and their bones, their skin and hair,

the brains in their heads, the food in their stomachs, the faeces
in their bowels, the urine in their bladders, their clothes, the money

in their pockets, the dirt on their shoes, as well as absolutely all
of the empty spaces inside the car are made entirely of chocolate.

The chocolaty smell that escapes from the car's body shell, is the perfume
worn by the chocolate woman who sits, completely engulfed in chocolate,

in the chocolate passenger seat. She's smiling to herself with chocolate lips
over chocolate teeth in a chocolate mouth that's crammed chock-full

of chocolate. She's smiling because she can sense that she's pregnant
with an embryo that's a minuscule, errant, miraculous bubble of air.

His Life Lost Him

Admit that you found him under a certain gravity
of drink as he fingered his heart, as he coined

his shiny innards one by one and spoke them all
until he had none.

And what has he done with his bones, the aerials
that should pick up the self and its attendant flesh?

His emptiness makes him nauseous and he can't
bring it up to be full again.

He declares that though he has no anchoring of weight,
he cannot be a vacancy, because he breathes,

and this creamy breath of his, he says, is the
gist of everything that lives, and only when

it's squeezed from a living thing, as an affecting tone
might be squashed from a squeeze box,

or a bee's buzz pushed from the busby of its body,
only then is the creature emptied. Say, at least,

that you share an understanding; say that it was you,
in fact, who spun him from the stuffing of him.

The Arctic Circle is an Ironical Hot-Spot

The North Pole is surrounded by Inuits who can't tell the difference
between a tennis racquet and a snow shoe. That is an Inuit joke.

These people live their whole lives ironically whereas down here
in the so-called developed world we've become somewhat distrustful

of irony and feel uncomfortable when we notice any, just as we do
when we hear the sound of the Earth grinding its black back teeth.

To us irony seems un-organic and unwholesome. It smells of disinfectant,
and we now know that germs are good for us. To the Inuit irony is still

so fashionable because it reached them comparatively recently,
and now that's it's there, it seems to thrive in the cold temperatures

and looks great set against the minimalism of a mostly white backdrop.
The Inuit plan is this: never to run away from irony but, on the contrary,

to go so far into it that they come out the other side into a fresh kind
of universe that doesn't seem all tired and past it and suspect

and found-out. They believe they'll find their beautiful wives
and their sons waiting for them there, with stars floating in their eyes again.

Some Time Afterwards

Perhaps it was a sense he had
of missing something which made him realise

he'd handed her a weightless ball
of complicated moving light,

which looked, admittedly, very like
a special effect from that period.

It was of a size that would slip perfectly
into her palm (every slip is Freudian),

and when she looked down it lit her face
in a way that was reminiscent of a scene in a film.

The rest of the world's light seemed then,
and still seems now, unaffected by what he did.

There is so much that is real,
such an abundance of it, that a tiny piece

of innocent spell like this is sanctioned
by the usually stern laws that govern things.

Everyone, even I, turned away
so he could give her his glowing, analogous stone.

The Limpet

An limpet sticks, just as we shift itchily.
The cow groans, just as we play our banjos
with an solemnity to which they are unsuited.
The stone is shut-up
while traditionally we bemoan
our jejune outfits and shudder
that we were given an scratchy voice. The ants,

the ants are polished, hideously well made,
spick, span, just as we are dun and underdone
and overdone. The cat is, to a great extent,
fur, while we are innovative.
The bird is beaked, us totally squeaked-off
with our elegant speech. I misheard you
underneath an cloud, under all that is implicit.

A Fire Itself is Quiet

A fire is quiet, though the burned,
will crack and pop and bang
and whistle ironically, as though
not reacting to their destruction, but to
a piping bath or to the heat of a hot day.

The margin and the tip
are the spicier portions of a flame;
a fire's leaves, like the leaves of a nettle,
sting and blister most at that serrated edge.
But beneath the new growth of these

excitable extremities, back where the fire
is more at ease, its heat is rank and cold.
The whole catastrophe is made up
down here, where ash collects, some little way
behind the excitation of the young blades.

Everything

The inside, as I recall, is furnished, wallpapered—
any smallish pattern.

The admirable day (though the pale blue sky is imbecilic)
is shown through the windows.

Above the flowers, honey bees
are in any number of positions again and again,

and the trees, though wooden, though peachy,
can't help but display their leaves, each one of which

is like, though unlike, a hand. Everything throngs on her tongue
as she throngs on mine. What's not to like?

Your Hand

Your own hand is more your old friend
than your own face is, your face
which looks to you a hustling fool,

which keeps between its skull and skin
its own unreadable thoughts, your face
that is no longer pleased nor sad for you.

Your hand is like a small boy who stands
in the thin, white dust on the edge
of the haggling crowd and waits for you.

The Warehouse

This is not a false alarm. This is not a drill.
This is an emergency. It's not just *about* an emergency.
It's not just *on the subject* of an emergency,
it doesn't merely *refer to* some emergency
that's taking place elsewhere. Neither is it
a metaphor for an emergency, or an exclamation
drawing attention to an emergency.
It is actually *the* emergency, and it requires attention.
It's not so much like a fire in a warehouse
where paper is stored, ordered by colour and weight
and finish and size, ordered by shape and age;
it's more like a fire in a warehouse built for the storage of fire.
The fire can make nothing of its heat inside its burning home.

Take a Gulp of Air

and dunk your shrunken head inside
a Harry's pocket what's half full of jokes
and the stuff he can't recognise and the so-called felt-up,
feel-good squirt of it all. (Every 'arry, by the way,
has a ludic one that labours, stunned and half-cut

beneath its own pomp.) Then find a sixteenth century cottage
that's nestled in a crater on the black and white moon,
a cottage where the woodworms and the moths
did suffocate for want of a more involved story,
and where gravity has an insouciant manner which grates.

Now, take a little time to watch the full moon loll,
cottage side up, in the pocket's dirt-dimmed light,
and you'll find there the selfsame indisposition
what I have been bequeathed: this jam-stuffed hollow
that stands salutin' in the hole.

I Can Use my Mouth

I can utilise my mouth;
I can make it suck or say *dum-de-dum*,
or whatever, seeing as it's at my beck,

seeing as it certainly seems to be slave
to my wishes. I might put food inside
the livid bouche-hole, *thus, thus*; perhaps

tomato, potato. The food then powers
the wobbly beak, and out of it comes
tomato, potato, and out of it comes

what it says. It says, I quote, *my teeth,
they're twice pushed out beyond my gums,
and stand halfway to death, bare to the suck*

*and blow, recording its number; white to my
earth-coloured drone; hard and stiff before that
which is all soft and accommodation.*

It mentions how it's me who fabricates
the spit I spit into my own mouth
to lubricate it, to keep it wet, just as I'm

kept muggy in this skin-tent I camp in,
propped with its struts of bone. In fact
my mouth is gagging to talk,

it intends to squeal, it means to finger me
with its jabbing tongue, to point me out
in the crowd and shop me. Yes,

the countenance's loose blowhole, it wants
to bite the very hand that feeds it, and spill
the beans. So I'll shut it

inside the box of its face; I shan't let it
either gas or mutter; I'll set it to kiss or lick
or dribble; I'll set it to hum or whistle.

So, I heard and also dreamed,

and I made up and I guessed and I gleaned that they ensconced
the clever thing or insensate thing or things in the hut in the woods,
in the old mine in the hill and in the sweating boathouse down
by the shore (the shore, as they put it, of the soaking sea;
the sea of which no single sheaf yet found, is dry

to the touch; because the wet cannot be wrung, or spun from it).
So they put the brute, or brutes, or mademoiselle, or lump of rock
(or nothing at all, they'd sometimes have us believe) twice
or maybe many times in all of these places (as well as some
or maybe many others) and then they purposely forgot

which place they'd left it in, and tried to forget (and maybe did)
that they'd left it at all. *The gentleman, it slid about,* they one time said.
They said it was embossed with leaf and stick and flower,
or they said she was engraved, or there were two of them or more,
engaged one unto another, and that he stitched his creasing body,

or seemed to, or certainly might have done. Our papas then
(inside our mamas' knowing) left it. And too afraid and thrilled,
they were, to look on it again; too afraid and happy to see it living,
and certainly to see it dead with this stretched grimace on its face,
and we pray it died and getting up, quietly did carry off its shame

as well as its own bones with it, and we know it died and carried off
this shame with it, and didn't dig out through the floor, or stay
and live its life inside and feed itself on the thick-thin gravy
of that shame. And none of us will even look towards those places,
or go near enough to hear no noise from them again.

Mallards

Before the aquatic show, with the flooded stage
and the water lilies, the ducks leave their hushful bills

in the cloakroom, in order to avoid being objects
of ridicule while they're sat in the auditorium,

just as we leave our bunched and delicate secrets hidden
down each other's underwear,

secrets which are very like the stiffening
and tightening sensation of a smile that pushes back

our malleable cheeks. It's later, in the back room,
that the cloakroom attendants do not clack

the ducks' deposited bills like castanets, for their own
amusement. It doesn't even occur to them.

Of Plants

fig i. There are so many tiny holes
that the chunks of the sun dot-permeate.

The chlorophyll donates an electron,
a ball, a little wave.

fig ii. The border is meanwhile herbaceous.
Flower, the Universe congealed into these nodes,

the Universe bunched about the stopping stems.
If I could find you here

among these just-so positioned heads it would be so!
It was once. Yes, I did once find you,

all your skin petal, moments ago.

fig iii. Now it's dusk. Time turns with its wooden smell
and the plant is scaffold to the swinging quiet.

An old man stands outside his cottage,
his impudent ghost escaping from the chimney behind him.

fig iv. Allow me? Oh, you could give me my life again?

To change one dog to one cat

you perhaps ought to take yourself
to the park at a convenient time
of your particular choosing.
You should find there what may be a dog,
knowing it by its humour.
Take it home. Then, fast on the ready table,
siphon its yap (you can do this);
then on the washed table,
stick it with a shameful enslavement to mice;
in the drawing room, on cushions,
make it to fathom slowly and then quick
that it is not itself; disconnect
(with a straightforward yank) its crush on booze
and the chew of the meaty cigarettes
and the grunt of the trundling ground.
So, first ordain it a fish —
cat being fish, dog being fished.
Make sure to bend it, as well, to a pale,
dusty blue before you plead it,
and if needs be, require it to black,
and to show what you've done,
make it to whistle itself, once if you like.

And see

how almost immediately this particular event
has begun to set hard in the crunchy track

that's always unfurling like the imprint of a thick
reptilian tail behind the jumpy and nitwitted present.

The splashiness of the precise present
precedes that stage of egg-white-like consistency

it's achieving here, as it's first beginning to trudge
into the sideburned and costive past,

while it whistles its self-consciously innocent tune
(that warbling ditty of the departing now

that's reminiscent of the sound of an infant's musical toy).
The disconcerting, transitional state is only

a brief one though, for it is very promptly that this,
or any other moment, will be muffled and will begin

to settle down, just as a small boy will settle down,
his features solidifying somewhat on approaching

the soporific gloom of a classroom with its
attendant faint reek of the mature that leaks out

of a teacher and is suggestive of an opprobrious
1950s secret or some sophisticated delicacy

which a child would spit into its mother's loving hand
(though the child, nonetheless, will entertain

a memory of a liking for its grown-up odour —
as though at the moment of its conception the cell

had split into a pair of nostrils which had smelt
the parents' sex. An adult smell which the child

will associate thereafter with this very first waking
which takes place nine long months before the curtains

are finally drawn with that slow flourish. It's that
inaugural waking surely, that is the punch line

to the shaggy dog story of our previous, eternal death.)
So, where were we? Indeed, where are we? Right here

at the edge of this particular paragraph, looking back
towards the one above, as though we stood

on the border of a wood and gazed across a strip
of grass towards another wood, already visited.

Right here where the moment first begins to set, to dry
and stiffen. A process which might seem to be complete

even at this very early stage and is achieved
in a surprisingly short period of time,

as the structure of what was once the present
starts to lose its integrity and begins to flake away

into dust or larger pieces of plaster-like matter.
Indeed, very soon, this here and now will be formed

entirely from an inert powder, a desiccated,
crumbled bygone, relating to its perky origins

not even to the extent that dried potato flakes
relate to their original potatoes. And this powder

of the past will require the soppingness of our own
future extants dressed up

in the quaint garb of the past and cut with our own
individual, particular

and specific 'seasoning' (that spice
that's shipped to us from the distant countries

of our precise histories) to be stirred vigorously into it
if it is to have any semblance of existence.

It's that spice surely, that always gives the past
this same regrettable flavour.

Iron

An iron is exactly like a dog—
a flat-bellied, hard and legless dog with neither bite

nor bark nor mouth, but with a tail
which may be plugged into a socket.

As it's moved across damp clothing, an iron is attached
to its user by an arm; that arm is like a dog's thick leash,

a leash that's attached to the shoulder
of someone with no arm. An iron is like a dog

that when it goes for a walk, never hesitates for long
in one place for fear of setting fire to the ground.

When its point is moved carefully around
an obstacle such as a button, an iron is like a dog

sniffing around another dog's genitals.
And when it's left to cool, an iron is like a dog

that rests on its rear end, its nonexistent eyes staring up
at the ceiling in amazement at its unlikely position.

I stood, preposterous

against the quiet and the night
and watched you lie

divested of your wakefulness
that lay in folded shreds

about my heavy feet.
And the part of you which sleeps

beneath the candy colour film
of you when you're awake,

I found awakened in your sleep
and it in turn awoke that ghost of me.

The Moon

He could recall the yellow coloured desks
and some of the ocean-going scale of the adult:

See here children, how the moon is held round.
It has hugged its own quantity so hard,

it has no arms no more.
The moon is dusty and without wind and that doesn't matter.

It heaves up the whole of the sea and lets it down again,
and up, and down,

and is our ventilator, and as the tides rise
they hide part of the glamorous earth from us

so that we hanker for more of her, and as it goes out
we become excited and behold one another

with flickery-clear faces as though we were hallucinations,
and without the tides we would become

uninterested in much at all and would spend all our time
waiting to be hungry.

Dawn

Cod-desperate gulls scream and draw
slow scribbles in the air above

the battered little boat that spills onto its pale deck
a hauled up catch that's all doused and black

and just before was breathing deep my blood.
Pulled, as each one is, from that particular soupy sea

of my rich and vulgar body, convergent evolution's
given every one of them the exact same

well-fed look as it begins to dry,
and the precise same light and also heavy sound

as it flapping, tries to swim half-heartedly
inside the wishy-washy realm of air.

Rooms

There is a long sadness about tables.
Drawing room furniture also has a forlorn quality,
but only the antique kind. Modern furniture,
on the contrary, possesses a certain carefree naivety
and an air of foolishness.
Dining chairs, and especially kitchen chairs
are also not unhappy, for any sorrow that may accrue
is shaken from them as they are moved about at every meal.
The doors, even the internal doors, have the slight aura
of aloofness possessed by those
who have some small degree of magical ability.
In common with the walls — even those hung
with the frivolity of wallpaper — floors have a certain attitude
of self possession. That includes the floors in kitchens
and certainly the ones in bedrooms, hallways, bathrooms,
and dining rooms, whether carpeted or otherwise.
Ceilings hang over each of them and always with the same
vacant air, which offers the floors no hope of having
their comparative worldliness reflected. The ceilings
give only what they can — the hygienic gaze of the retarded.

The Attributes of Cutlery

The knives, the forks and the spoons
each generally inhabit individual compartments,
with another fourth and perpendicular space
being allocated to the teaspoons
which, contrary to appearances,
are not junior relatives
to the more boorish dessert spoons,
but in fact carry an air of self importance
which is derived partly from the civilised
and civilising sound which they educe
from the otherwise restrained porcelain of saucers,
but also from their more temperate appetites
as well as their apparent ability
to measure their contents with more precision
than that achieved by any of the larger members
of that family. The knives are artless;
they possess neither the congenital guile
of the spoons, nor the quiet dubiety of the forks.

I could certainly see you better,

no doubt because the setting was unfamiliar,
the way the water sluices the gutters
in the mornings, for example; how it carries
your imagination helplessly under the ground.

That doesn't happen back here. The effect
is similar to when you move a painting
from one room to another and find you can
see it vividly again, at least for a while; or when

age moves over your own face and you realise
that you're not just a gust of air after all,
and that all those ordinary events like death
that happen to other people, will happen to you.

I have photographs I took in cafes in Paris;
they bring back at least some of that clarity.
You're looking at me with an expression
you sometimes had then which alluded

to the physical space between us and to tiny,
imaginary versions of ourselves who stood
in that space nearly amused by the two of us,
as though indulgent of their irascible parents.

I won't say our life together crawled up
out of the ground wearing its full costume,
like a body dipped in its face, or even that trees
spoke quite clearly in French. But I will say

that I want you to forgive me for this
fanciful tone which I know I have adopted.
It is the card I find I always play in response
to the way you look at me in the photographs.

Of Course, We've All Seen This Kind of Thing Before

The missile is decorated in thick paint which depicts
an eighteenth century hunting scene.

The intended effect is a frisson of irony
that might move through consciousness

in a ripple resembling a fading chuckle. In flight,
the paint's bumpy embossments trouble the air editorially,

as the pins on a music box's turning drum trouble
the steel comb's teeth (those pins which are like men

on a cylindrical world — men who play always their singular note
according to their position).

The missile is carbon neutral; its exhaust fumes are offset
by the planting of ideas in the minds of the viewers who,

being afraid of dying, and therefore
susceptible to cheap jokes, hold tight their helpless breaths.

When You Do This Over and Over

After a little while you'll find there's a wall you come up against.
You might press your hands and your cheek against it

and scrape at it with your spade but you won't breach it.
(Nowadays we believe the wall is made of what was done to us

when we were so small and new as to be quite easily torn.)
Once you've got some measure of this barrier you'll discover

that everything you do, no matter how you might twist and turn,
will be done on this side of it, even though what's beyond

is no more than the continuation of yourself. Everything you do
will look OK certainly, but not *entirely* OK.

It might seem as smart or cod-jejune or arch or cod-arch
or cod-cod as you like and absolutely it will be true, but still,

it will begin to grate on you. In short, your actions will begin
to find themselves embarrassing;

they will be ashamed of their position here, outside the perimeter
of what everyone knows is the main event.

Lion

Though a lion may appear to be strokeable,
its fur is, in fact, a lure, a seducement

developed in half-lit rooms by geeks,
a ruse with which they mean to charm our children

before stripping them of their edibleness with no regard
for the agony and shock

which that will cause them. And should they, one day,
find the means to give the lion speech,

then the beast will shed, as suddenly as if from shock,
its henceforth superfluous fur,

and then will take a little breath and lean across
the playground's fence, in its blue-grey skin, to talk.

Look at the trees which carry on regardless,

disclosing their leaves unashamedly
(as though they were nothing!) and letting the bark
take place around their trunks in the manner

of a grim chortle. All dust eventually comes down;
and on bedroom walls wallpaper crops up
and hangs on furiously.

Of course I'm know I'm guessing, but presumably
the ground pussyfoots beneath your feet
as it does beneath mine,

or dumps itself, like a teenager,
sullenly underneath you, as it does under me.
I'm assuming that if you have

a tucked-in holy ghost, he stands out there
on the lip of his existence while you watch him,
avec the whole of your falutin' mouth dug out.

Defenestration

A sheet of glass is always a barrier to sound
and will gag our flickering mouths

or plug our nosey ears far more fully
than noise will be muffled by an earmuff.

A frame's gaping hole can only mime its pane,
and, shattered, glass will multiply and fall as leaves

will fall before the opened winds of winter.
Even its smallest fragments are chameleons which

can hold the expression of the place they're in
across the uncertain faces of their bodies,

for these vengeful fragments, the offspring
of the smitten window, reveal what would be there

if they were not. Until, that is, they're doused
in sudden blood, when they'll be read as shock.

Well yes, where we interface

there certainly are wobbles—the fit not being perfect.
This strangeness comes from there,

partly from the shock of finding it forced on us
and partly from finding

it's not as natural to us as death is.
Where we press up upon our living

there are jolts,
so that we might seem to stick for a moment

and then jump lurchingly
as continental plates do, catastrophically sometimes,

and when you meet someone, in the street perhaps,
even someone you know, whole large chunks of them

might be torn away by this effect
and roll to the side of the road

and you'll be shouting at them somewhere
in an absolutely murdered voice, and them at you.

The darking sky

was like a fashionable woman of a certain age
whose long fingered hand

rests, for a moment motionless,
on a restaurant table's tablecloth, and which

some uncertain time before had held a snub,
part-grown and uninvented pigling pig

whose temperature and incantatory scent
still slumbers happy in her partly parted grasp.

Skin is the callus

formed on the wet
and bauble-shiny insides by the gritty wind,

by the hot and the dry and the cold.
The daylight troubles innards too,

as it does the glossy mole, the spittled worm,
the blind, uncoloured troglobite;

it glimmers on the organs' half-meant membranes
as they lie jostling one another,

afraid beneath the frightened peep of eyes:
those hunkered scouts whose role it is

to push their shiny faces beyond the curtain's
velvet shroud. Now take this, my purplish heart

in your skin-gloved hand again and hurt it
with your sweat's pretty sting.

If I was,

I don't know, walking down, say, a street
and I happened to come across

a group of, I don't know, firemen
who were fighting, say, a fire,

then I might imagine, might I not,
their fire hose to be a long and beige salami.

And then I might imagine, might I not,
that I could take a slice of that salami,

that I could peel it of its ring of canvas skin
and then I'd have a lens,

the freshest monocle through which,
if I held it to my open eye, I'd probably see

a group of firemen with a cut hose
shouting angrily.

Uncertain Voices Roost

The six I counted,
rooks that fly from the single window
at the top of the tall and pale tower,
are each your voice that wheels and turns about.

In your un-shuttered mouth the clever fowl
make up their brittle nests of sticks
and lay their clever eggs whose shells
each taste of the birding earth.

In that damp, abandoned home, fledgling chicks
will hatch and tug on the glossy worms that hang
from the wet ceiling at the back of the little room.
The feathered voices peck uncaringly at us.

Inside

Just as water is disturbed by shifts in temperature,
so my interior is disturbed by alterations in my behaviour.
She adjusts herself; she lines herself up accordingly
and experiences all the actions I choose to make, positive
or negative, receives all the food or other substances
I ingest, as having no intentionality behind them,
or in the same way as I might experience the weather.
She receives what's given, not graciously or ungraciously,
but as a foetus or a small child would, accepting whatever
I dole out. Despite all this, my inside is happier with her lot
than I am with this position of mine as an undone man.

She barely senses my discomfort, and though she does feel
my temper, it is only as a curdling that's akin to a primitive
kind of pleasure, perhaps to the extent, at least, that a leaf
takes a kind of pleasure in the warmth of the sun. At night,
she's content to be the sole witness to her own noise,
a murmuring as unorganised by any intelligence as the grind
of the gears of the earth when they shift, in their stupor, against
one another. She's as completely believing as the shopping
I lug home in a bag, and of course can't know that she will die
some brief moment before me, or how I will need to mourn,
for that instant, the loss of her weight.

Observe the likeness of a slab of beef

to a neckerchief. The first going down your neck,
the second, slipping round it.

And how dissembling memory is resemblant
of a slice of brie, that reaches pungent puberty

as its sudden curves spill from white clothes
just before we fall

so ravenously on it. And how akin
are the chastened living and the bumptious dead,

sharing as they do these pleasant bones, these teeth
I find in my mouth that I find in my head.

And isn't strawberry kindred to this girlish hope of mine
and isn't a small child like a small stone

in a small wood
where the ripe and stinking tramps are making rhymes

from the nasty likenesses of things
and setting up their homes in the still and silver mind.

The Sea

The sea, days out from shore,
here, where there's no other element
to throw and beat herself against

and then, withdrawing, drag herself against,
to leave the jagged rocks completely soaked
in her thin and bubbled blood;

here, in muddle-headed grief, she wrings
wet hands for all the fishermen
she couldn't help but wrap

in her soppy, over-the-top embrace.
Every salty tear shed only adds
to that terrible enormity, as her sorrow strives

to salt itself away in submerged caves,
(to hide itself even from me) and cry alone,
for all the boys whose clam-clenched lips

she, quite helpless, smooched and slobbered,
breached then wadded well with her unbudded,
huge, unbidden tongue.

Beef is Made of Meat and Victory

Chicken is made of fish,
fish is made of lettuce-like vegetable,
and vegetable is made of dirt or stone.

Man then is made of pig—
hog that stomps and tantrums and hollers
and inveigles itself into a man

before turning back to sulk the long,
long sulk, as the stars (which are themselves
—like everything that lives—made of dissatisfaction)

go out one by one,
just like that, and just like that.
The cold is made exclusively of itself.

The Petard

From the very off
my thinking has been muddled,
even before the unprepared departure
with all that unnecessary luggage
from my so-called 'Parisian apartment'
in (lazily) a gondola,

and certainly here, at my destination,
as I look out across
what I'm referring to as 'The Atlantic Sea'
yes definitely here, as I gaze out
from this spot in western France
which I've constructed for the purpose
of gazing out from it.

For I find that now I'm on the beach,
my leather suitcases around me,
the sand running through my fingers,
and the sea, literally, green, I'm lost.

I'm not so much adrift,
not so much afloat as sunk in that exact
leaky vessel in which I have so recently
embarked and been propelled
to this miserable spot by the idle gondolier
of whim (or the furtive gondolier
of who knows what
strange unconscious purpose).

And I find myself not exactly hoisted
to some dizzy heights by the voluminous,
unfolding bang of my own well-packed petard,
as, *au contraire*, dragged down
by the steady dread of it.

Make Use of My Poem in Any Way You Like

Make an origami goose. Cut fine holes for the light
to glint though. Fabricate a paper chain of convivial men.

Make a dart, or a hat for a biggish bird or a cat.
Doodle freely in the margins if you will. Go ahead, jot

little notes on the more salient passages, cross-referencing
them with passages in other works of mine, picking up

on themes maybe, and noting how respectfully,
as well as snugly, it slips into a long-held-vacant slot

in the wider canon. (Notice, by-the-way how it somehow
seems to soften its important neighbours with an easy,

self-deprecating charm.) Make copies of it. Feel free.
Hand them out to special friends, maybe fold and slip them

into their shirt pockets saying something simple
and mysterious like, *Check it out*. Deconstruct it, help yourself.

Take it apart piece by polished piece, to see how it works,
to watch the keen little engine spin, lit with innocent heat.

Taste

However vulgar death
or serious injury may be
when they involve spilt
or sprayed arterial blood,
they are brief and rare
enough events, looked at
in the context of the span
of the average life,
as to represent only a tiny
splash of garish colour
on what is otherwise
a largely subdued canvas.
Our excreta, for example,
are not at all brightly
coloured. Piss is pale.
And the subdued,
Rembrandtesque hues
of faeces can be queasily
observed, squeezed
from the bowel's tube
onto the porcelain bowl's
bright palette. Tellingly,
our secretions, such as
saliva and sweat and tears
are also soft in tone.
Semen too is famously
just off-white,
the wall colour of a
modernist architect's
apartment. And an aroused
woman's emanations

are transparent; glossy,
certainly, but tastefully so,
as the varnish
on a mahogany handrail.

Rude

as though outside under a
charred sky that's the lifted bun

of a burger that's like the wet, new road
at night and like the filthy dirt

and the windowless body of a cow
and the frantic kissing

of these competent plants,
their petals bruised and shaky

and so, so nude to your pilfered look—
as is this spit-shone,

rubbed-up stomp inside my bosom.
O egg of stiffening greed.

And there he is again,

the boy detective, hurrying along
on the other side of the gloomy street.

To look at him, you'd think that underneath
his green cloak, against his scribbled stomach,
he clutched a medium-sized box of heavy wood,
plain or inlaid with brass or ivory,
and that in that box was a pearl, though tiny;
small as the abdomen of an ant

or else enormous as a croquet ball that leaves
only a millimetre's space between its own border
and the internal walls of the box it's in
so that it rattles hardly at all, and then
only with a soft and deep knocking
like some despairing signal.

And then it is
that all the world's ordinary sized pearls,
(that rest on the greyish pillows
of their oysters' flesh, like gallstones lounging
in their kidneys, or parade with their neighbours
on the plush cushions of their owners' bosoms,
like toy soldiers marching on sprung floors)
smile pleased and brittle little smiles,
because all these humdrum pearls divine
that the monster pearl's absurd, and will not
be entertained, shall not be authorised.

And so they watch as its and every value
judders only for an instant before the brittle laws
that govern us locate the aberration
and soon the smoke of non-computing starts
to emanate from it and then to satiate
what little space is left inside the box,

though a wisp of smoke, crisp and broken
as a snail's trail, and invisible to us, rises
from the cask's keyhole to rasp the fellow's
nostrils as he breaks into his scamper,
his lush cloak swarming, as he almost achieves
the left hand frame of the little scene he's,
just for this moment, still a part of.

Grub

The maggot is the uncooked fly,
the raw, the pale mixture that stirs itself
in the scalloped bowl of its body
and from which the browning bug
will rise and dry and taking in the air
lose its puppy weight.

The future hairy adult's heat
reaches back to bake
its former maggot into it. Or it's time
that turns and, moving in reverse,
scrubs off the wings, the brittle limbs,
erodes the crusty fly into its worm.

Poem for Us

We are more evolved
than the hogs are. We have shed much more

of our hair in order to become more streamlined,
prettier on the eye and lickable/tasteable.

We've left the dirt, from which we all came,
further and further behind till it's near over the horizon

(there is no dirt in space, our ultimate destination, surely).
We then make good use of the hog

for various 'other purposes'. Such as, one:
we rub ourselves against them, using the hog hair

as a kind of scourer to smooth ourselves off with;
two: we use the porker's itchy smell as a comparison

with our own more dinky odours; three:
we utilise their grunt as a dirty mirror in which to see

our own sweet hum. (And four, we eat 'em,
wasting nothing). Upon times, we make use of fish too.

We catch them from the pond in our many fingers,
then we look them in the eye to see

their own non-blink looking back at us,
and to feel this, our own caught weight, not struggling.

In the end,

we are so sad under the trees,
so crushed beneath notions,

lorn and lost and left to ourselves
by the idling angels, so cute and so wild,

so fit with their glory,
their manicured aspects, their infant cuticles,

their clothes torn up with their glory.
And we are bound under gooseflesh,

once stripped and then born, the sky, ragged.
We are under the world from which

might reach only the hands of the inklings
that strum but scraps of tune on us.

The Porcelain Dog

The porcelain dog,
despite his unruffled exterior,
despite his apparent serenity,
suffocates for want inside
his tight and glossy bag of glaze,
and so it is with me,
beneath this painted sack
that is my cloak of visibility.

Lightning Source UK Ltd.
Milton Keynes UK
UKHW020732261119
354261UK00007B/277/P